To My Daughter

with Love
on the Important
Things in Life

ISBN: 978-1-68088-070-0

◼ and Blue Mountain Press are registered in U.S. Patent and Trademark Office. Certain trademarks are used under license.

Printed in China.
First Printing: 2016

♻ This book is printed on recycled paper.

This book is printed on paper that has been specially produced to be acid free (neutral pH) and contains no groundwood or unbleached pulp. It conforms with the requirements of the American National Standards Institute, Inc., so as to ensure that this book will last and be enjoyed by future generations.

Blue Mountain Arts, Inc.

P.O. Box 4549, Boulder, Colorado 80306

To My Daughter
with Love
on the Important
Things in Life

Susan Polis Schutz

Illustrated by
Stephen Schutz

Blue Mountain Press™
Boulder, Colorado

To My Daughter, with Love

My day becomes wonderful
when I see your
pretty face smiling so sweetly
There is such warmth and intelligence
radiating from you
It seems that every day
you grow smarter and more beautiful
and every day
I am more proud of you
As you go through different stages of life
you should be aware that there will be many times
when you will feel scared and confused
but with your strength and values
you will always end up wiser
and you will have grown from your experiences
understanding more about people and life
I have already gone through
these stages
So if you need advice or someone to talk to
to make sense out of it all
I hope that you will talk to me
as I am continually cheering for your happiness
my sweet daughter
and I love you

I Have So Many Wishes for You

I wish for you to have
people to love
people in your life
who will care about you
     as much as I do
blue skies and clear days
exciting things to do

I wish for you to have
easy solutions to any problems
knowledge to make the right decisions
strength in your values
laughter and fun
goals to pursue
happiness in all that you do

I wish for you to have
beautiful experiences
each new day
as you follow
your dreams

You Can Always Depend on Me

I looked at you today
and saw the same beautiful eyes
that looked at me with love
when you were a baby

I looked at you today
and saw the same beautiful mouth
that made me cry when you first smiled at me
when you were a baby
It was not long ago
that I held you in my arms
long after you fell asleep
and I just kept rocking you
all night long
I looked at you today
and saw my beautiful daughter
no longer a baby
but a beautiful person
with a full range of emotions
feelings, ideas and aspirations
Every day is exciting
as I continue to watch you grow
I want you to always know that
in good and in bad times
I will love you
and that no matter what you do
or how you think
or what you say
you can depend on
my support, guidance
friendship and love
every minute of every day

This Is for Those Times When You Just Need to Know That Someone Cares

Sometimes we do not feel
like we want to feel
Sometimes we do not achieve
what we want to achieve
Sometimes things happen
that do not make sense
Sometimes life leads us in directions
that are beyond our control
It is at these times, most of all
that we need someone
who will quietly understand us
and be there to support us

I want you to know
that I am here for you
in every way
and remember that though
things may be difficult now
tomorrow is a new day

I Love You So Much, My Beautiful Daughter

I wish that you could see yourself
as others see you —
a sensitive, pretty, loving, intelligent person
who has all the qualities necessary to
become an outstanding woman
Yet sometimes you seem to
have a low opinion of yourself
You compare yourself unfavorably to others
I wish that you would only judge yourself
according to your own standards
and not be so hard
on yourself
I look forward to the day
when you look in the mirror
and for the first time in your life
you see the extraordinary person
that you really are
and you realize how much
you are loved and appreciated
I love you so much
my beautiful daughter
forever as your mother
and friend

Sometimes you
think that you
need to be perfect
that you cannot
make mistakes
At these times
you put so much
pressure on yourself

I wish that you
would realize
that you are
like everyone else —
capable of
reaching great potential
but not capable of
being perfect
So please
just do your best
and realize that
this is enough
Be happy to be
the wonderful
unique, very special
person that you are

Only You Can Choose the Lifestyle You Want to Follow

We cannot
listen to what
others want us
to do
We must listen
to ourselves

We don't need to
copy other people's ways
and we don't need to
act out certain lifestyles
to impress other people
Only we know
and only we can do what
is right for us
So start right now
You will need to
work very hard
You will need to
overcome many obstacles
You will need to go
against the better
judgment of many people
and you will need to
bypass their prejudices
But you can have
whatever you want
if you try hard enough
Start right now so that
you can live a life
designed by you and
for you —
a life you deserve

To My Daughter
with Love
on the Important
Things in Life

A mother tries to provide her daughter
with insight
into the important things in life
in order to make her life
as happy and fulfilling as possible

A mother tries to teach her daughter
to be good, always helpful to other people
to be fair, treating others equally
to have a positive attitude
to make things right when they are wrong
to know herself well
to know what her talents are
to set goals for herself
to not be afraid of working too hard to reach
her goals...

(continued)

A mother tries to teach her daughter
to have many interests to pursue
to laugh and have fun every day
to appreciate the beauty of nature
to enter into friendships with good people
to honor their friendships and always be
    a true friend
to appreciate the importance of the family
and to particularly respect and love our
    elder members
to use her intelligence at all times
to listen to her emotions
to adhere to her values

A mother tries to teach her daughter
to not be afraid to stick to her beliefs
to not follow the majority when the
    majority is wrong
to always realize that she is a woman
    equal to all men
to carefully plan a life for herself
to vigorously follow her chosen path
to enter into a relationship with someone
    worthy of herself
to love this person unconditionally with
    her body and mind
to share all that she has learned in life
    with this person

If I have provided you with an insight
into most of these things
then I have succeeded as a mother
in what I hoped to accomplish in raising you
If some of these things slipped by
while we were all so busy
I have a feeling that you know them anyway
And I certainly hope that you always
    continue to know
how much love and admiration
I have for you
my beautiful daughter

What Is
a Daughter?

A daughter is
a rainbow bubble
a star glimmering in the sky
a rosebud after a storm
a caterpillar turning into a butterfly

A daughter is
hair flying in the wind
red cheeks that glisten in the sunshine
big daydream eyes

A daughter is
a wonder
a sweetness, a secret, an artist
a perception, a delight

You are all these things
and so much more
You are everything that is beautiful

Daughter
when you were born
I held you in my arms
and just kept smiling at you
You always smiled back
your big eyes wide open
full of love
You were such an
angelic
good
sweet baby

Now
as I watch you grow up
and become your own person
I look at you
your laughter
your happiness
your simplicity
your beauty
And I know that you will
be able to enjoy a life
of sensitivity, goodness
accomplishment and love
I want to tell you that
I am so proud of you
and I dearly
love you

Every Mother Dreams of Having a Daughter like You

*y*ou are such an outstanding person
and I hope nothing ever changes
your inner beauty
As you keep growing
remember always
to look at things the way you do now —
with sensitivity
honesty
compassion
and a touch of innocence
Remember that people and situations
may not always be
as they appear
but if you remain true to yourself
it will be all right
With your outlook, you will see
the good in everything
and this will reflect back to you
When I look ahead
I see happiness for you on every level
and I am so glad
because that is what every mother
wishes for her daughter

I Will Always
Be Cheering
for Your Success

As you keep growing and learning
striving and searching
it is very important
that you pursue your own interests
without anything holding you back

It will take time
to fully understand yourself
and to discover what you want out
    of life
I know that the steps in your journey
will take you on the right path
Whatever happens in the future
I will always be cheering
for your happiness and success
and you can always depend
on my love and support

Find Happiness in Everything You Do

A woman will get only what she seeks
Choose your goals carefully
Know what you like
and what you do not like
Be critical about what you can do well
and what you cannot do well

Choose a career or lifestyle that interests you
and work hard to make it a success
but also have fun in what you do
Be honest with people
    and help them if you can
but don't depend on anyone
    to make life easy or happy for you
(only you can do that for yourself)
Be strong and decisive
but remain sensitive
Regard your family, and the idea of family
as the basis for security, support and love
Understand who you are
and what you want in life
before sharing your life with someone
When you are ready to enter a relationship
make sure that the person is worthy of
everything you are physically and mentally
Strive to achieve all that you want
Find happiness in everything you do
Love with your entire being
Love with an uninhibited soul
Make a triumph
of every aspect
of your life

Live Your World of Dreams

Lean against a tree
and dream your world
   of dreams
Work hard at what you like to do
and try to overcome all obstacles

Laugh at your mistakes
and praise yourself for
    learning from them
Pick some flowers
and appreciate the beauty of nature
Be honest with people
and enjoy the good in them
Don't be afraid to show your emotions
Laughing and crying make you feel better
Love your friends and family
    with your entire being
They are the most important part of
    your life
Feel the calmness on a quiet sunny day
and plan what you want to accomplish
    in life
Find a rainbow
and live your
world of dreams

My little daughter
(but no longer little)
As you grow into a young adult —
a bouquet of exquisite, vigorous flowers
and I look at you with awe…

Drink enough water of life
so you passionately blossom
When it is dark and cloudy
know that light will soon
shine through a clear sky

Absorb enough sunshine
to keep you warm
Absorb enough wind to flood you
with free-flowing movements

My young adult daughter
(but no longer little)
The fragrance of your world
will guide you
And I look at you with love

You are a shining
example of what a
daughter can be —
loving and compassionate
honest and principled
determined and independent
sensitive and intelligent
You are a shining
example of what every
mother wishes her
daughter were
You have made it
easy for me
to be a parent

Daughter,
I'm So Proud of You,
and I Love You

To see you happy —
laughing and dancing
smiling and content
striving toward goals of your own
accomplishing what you set out to do
having fun alone and with your friends
capable of loving and being loved
is what I have always wished for you

Today I thought about your beautiful face
and felt your excitement for life
and your genuine happiness
and I am so proud of you as I realize that
my dreams for you have come true
What an extraordinary person you are
and as you continue to grow
please remember always
how very much
I love you

About the Author and Artist

Susan Polis Schutz is an accomplished writer, poet, and documentary filmmaker. She is the author of many best-selling books of poetry illustrated by her husband, Stephen Schutz, including *To My Daughter with Love on the Important Things in Life*, which has sold over 1.8 million copies, and *To My Son with Love*, which has sold over 530,000 copies. Susan's latest undertaking is creating documentary films that make a difference in people's lives with her production company, IronZeal Films. Her films have been shown on PBS stations throughout the country and include *The Misunderstood Epidemic: Depression*, which seeks to bring greater attention to this debilitating illness; *Over 90 and Loving It*, which features people in their 90s and 100s who are living extraordinary and passionate lives; and *Anyone and Everyone*, which features a diverse group of parents and their gay children discussing their experiences. Her newest film, *It's Just Anxiety?*, provides a very honest and insightful look at the various forms of anxiety and the ways people have tried to overcome their anxiety.

Stephen Schutz has a PhD in Physics from Princeton University and is an accomplished photographer and calligrapher. In addition to designing and illustrating all of Susan's books, he is the genius behind bluemountain.com — the Internet greeting card service he created and cofounded with the help of his and Susan's eldest son, Jared. He is also the founder of starfall.com, an interactive website where children have fun while learning to read. In 2015, the Polis-Schutz family donated their full interest in starfall.com to the Starfall Education Foundation after supporting the project as a social enterprise for fifteen years.

In 1970, Susan and Stephen cofounded Blue Mountain Arts, a popular publisher known for its distinctive greeting cards, gifts, and poetry books. Susan's poems and Stephen's artwork have been published on over 435 million greeting cards worldwide.